Your Body and Health

BREATHING

Jen Green

STARGAZER BOOKS

Produced by: Aladdin Books Ltd

*First published in the
United States in 2006 by:*
Stargazer Books
c/o The Creative Company
123 South Broad Street
P.O. Box 227
Mankato, Minnesota 56002

Printed in Malaysia

Editor: Katie Harker

Designer: Simon Morse

Illustrators: Aziz A. Khan, Simon Morse,
Rob Shone, Sarah Smith, Ian Thompson

Cartoons: Jo Moore

Certain illustrations have appeared in
earlier books created by Aladdin Books.

Medical editor: Dr. Hilary Pinnock

*Dr. Pinnock is a GP working in England. She
has written and consulted on a wide variety
of medical publications for all ages.*

*Library of Congress Cataloging-in-
Publication Data*

Green, Jen.
   Breathing / by Jen Green.
      p. cm.
   Includes index.
   ISBN 1-59604-054-8
      1. Respiration--Juvenile literature.
      I. Title.

QP121.G676 2005
612.2--dc22

2005042527

Contents

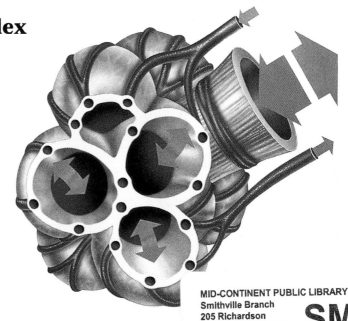

Introduction

Did you know that breathing is one of the most important processes in the human body? Taking air in and out of your lungs is essential to sustain life and to grow, move, and perform strenuous physical activities. The special process by which this occurs—the respiratory system—also enables you to do practical things like talking, singing, and blowing out candles. This book tells you all you need to know about your breathing system and how to keep it in good shape for a healthy body.

Medical topics

Use the red boxes to find out about different medical conditions and the effects that they can have on the human body.

You and your breathing

Use the green boxes to find out how you can help improve your general health and keep your respiratory system in good condition.

The yellow section

Find out how the inside of your body works by following the illustrations on yellow backgrounds.

Health facts and health tips

Look for the yellow boxes to find out more about the different parts of your body and how they work. These boxes also give you tips on how to keep yourself really healthy.

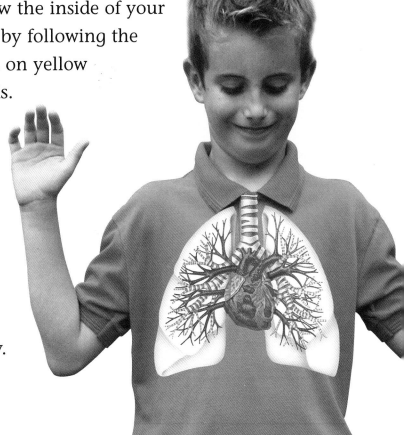

The respiratory system

Almost all living things need oxygen to flourish. This gas helps you to grow, and to process your food to give you the energy you need to move. Your lungs take oxygen from the air in a process called respiration (breathing). Humans can hold their breath for about a minute, but some animals, like whales, hold their breath for two hours!

Systems of the body

Breathing and circulation

Our bodies are often described in terms of separate systems, each with a different job to do. However, each body system is dependent on the others to work to its full potential. The respiratory system works closely with the circulatory system, which carries oxygen in the bloodstream from the lungs to the rest of the body.

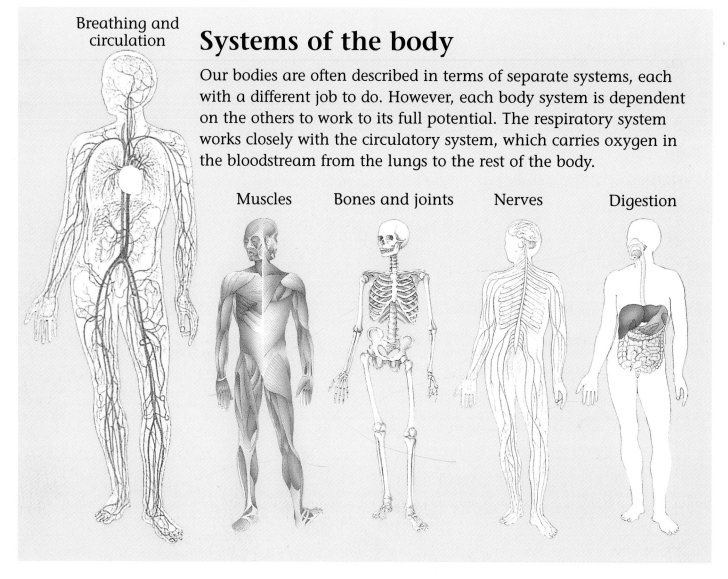

Muscles Bones and joints Nerves Digestion

Breathing is the key to many different processes in the body. When you talk, your breath passes through your windpipe and makes your vocal cords vibrate. You can make your voice louder or softer to shout, scream, or whisper by adjusting the force of the air that you breathe out.

Your breathing equipment

The body parts used in breathing are called the respiratory system. They include the nose and throat, the windpipe (or trachea), the breathing muscles, and the lungs. Your two lungs are located in your chest, one on either side of your heart. They are shaped like cones, with a narrow top and a wide base. The lungs have a spongy texture, and they work like sponges too, except that they absorb air, not water.

How it works

When you breathe in, air enters your mouth and nose and passes down your windpipe. Two smaller airways (bronchi) lead into smaller tubes (bronchioles) and air sacs. Oxygen passes through the walls of these sacs into your blood, which your heart pumps around your body. Waste gas (carbon dioxide) passes from the blood into the lungs, to be breathed out.

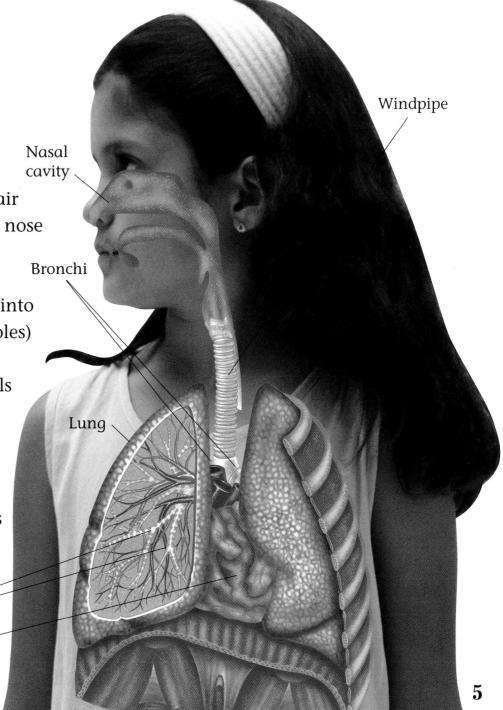

Windpipe

Nasal cavity

Bronchi

Lung

Bronchioles

Heart

The breath of life

Every time you breathe in, you fill your lungs with air, so that they inflate (swell) like a balloon. When you breathe out, stale air passes out of the lungs, so they deflate (shrink) again. During this process your lungs take oxygen from the air to be carried around the body in your blood. When you breathe out, your lungs get rid of carbon dioxide, which your body doesn't need.

Exercise such as swimming strengthens your breathing muscles and increases your stamina—your ability to keep going for a long time without collapsing in a heap!

Muscles need oxygen

Muscles work by pulling on bones, allowing you to perform all kinds of movements. As they work, muscles use up oxygen. The harder you exercise, the more oxygen your muscles need. This is why you breathe faster when you go for a bike ride.

Nonstop process

Try holding your breath. Your body can't store oxygen for much more than a minute. You need to keep breathing constantly, 24 hours a day, awake or asleep, to stay alive. If you hold your breath for a long time, your body will soon instinctively gasp for breath even if you don't want it to!

Where does oxygen come from?

Oxygen forms about 20 percent of the earth's atmosphere—the blanket of gases that surrounds our planet. Luckily for us, plants help to produce oxygen. Plants use energy from sunlight to make their food. The green parts of plants convert carbon dioxide, water, and minerals from soil into sugar, and oxygen is given off in the process. Oxygen can also be found in water and in the earth's crust.

Carbon dioxide

Light

Oxygen

Unlocking energy

Oxygen helps your body to unlock the energy that you can get from your food. Body cells use oxygen to break down food molecules, like sugar, to find the goodness they contain. This process releases energy which your body can use.

Lung protection

Your lungs are delicate organs that would be easily damaged if it weren't for your ribs, which form a protective cage around them. Your ribs are twelve pairs of flat, curving bones attached to your spine and to the long, straight breastbone (sternum) at the front of your chest. Your ribs also protect other delicate organs, such as your heart and liver.

Improving your breathing

Regular exercise makes your heart and breathing muscles fitter, so that they work more efficiently. Certain types of exercise, such as bike riding, jogging, and dancing, are particularly good for the heart and lungs, because they use up lots of oxygen.

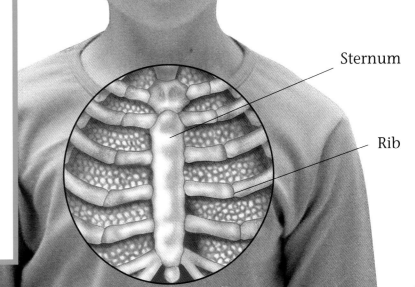

Sternum

Rib

Upper airways

The mouth, nose, and throat are your upper airways. Air flowing through your nostrils goes through the nasal cavity, a space inside your head, where the air is warmed and cleaned to remove dust and dirt. You can also breathe through your mouth. This is more common when you exercise because you can quickly inhale and exhale large quantities of air through your mouth.

Eating while you exercise is not a good idea, because food may go down the wrong way, making you choke!

Detecting smells

Your nose is also used for smelling. Two sensitive patches inside the top of your nose detect scent particles floating in the air. A sense of smell allows you to enjoy delicious scents, such as baking bread, flowers, and perfume. You can also notice smells that warn of danger, such as smoke from a fire. If you have a cold, or your nose is blocked, you will find it more difficult to smell.

Blowing your nose

Your nostrils and other airways are lined with a sticky fluid called mucus, which traps dust and dirt that you might breathe in. You clear the mucus by blowing your nose. When you get a cold your mucus-producing cells go into overdrive in an attempt to shed the virus.

Safety flap

Your throat contains two pipes—one for your food and the other for breathing. A stiff flap called the epiglottis in the throat makes sure everything "goes down the right way." As you swallow food, the epiglottis drops down to cover the windpipe. When the food is safely swallowed, the epiglottis flips up again to open the airways.

Breathing

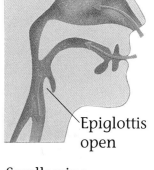

Epiglottis open

Swallowing

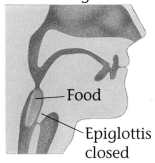

Food

Epiglottis closed

Upper air passages

Your nose and nostrils are mainly formed of gristly cartilage leading to a long cavity in the bones of your face. Both the nasal cavity and the mouth lead to your windpipe (or trachea). A knobbly lump called the Adam's apple lies at the top of the throat. It is part of your voice box (or larynx). Narrow passages called eustachian tubes lead from the nasal cavity to air chambers inside your ears.

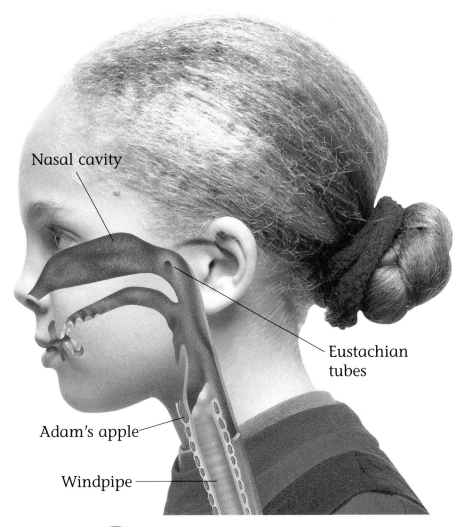

Nasal cavity

Eustachian tubes

Adam's apple

Windpipe

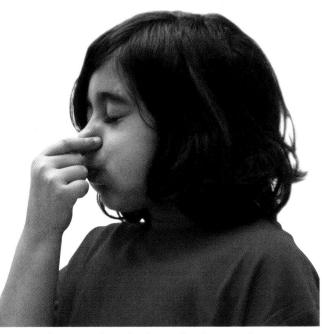

The eustachian tubes help to balance the air pressure inside your ears. If you have ever flown in an aircraft, your ears may have felt blocked or a bit uncomfortable. Swallowing, or blowing gently while holding your nose, helps to open your eustachian tubes. Your ears may gently "pop" as the air moves in or out to equalize the pressure.

Nosebleeds

The lining of your nose contains blood vessels that warm the air entering your nostrils. If your nose gets a hard knock, these vessels may tear and start to bleed. To stop a nosebleed, hold your head forward and gently squeeze the top of your nose. Breathe normally through your mouth. The blood will clot to seal the leak.

Inside the lungs

Your left lung is slightly smaller than your right lung, to leave space for your heart on the left side of your chest. Your lungs are stretchy and spongy because they are made of millions of tiny pipes and air-filled bubbles, too small for the eye to see. When you breathe in and out, air travels up and down these tiny air passages, where it is processed by your body.

Although the air sacs in your lungs are tiny, they add up to a huge surface area. If flattened out, they would cover an area the size of a tennis court.

Inside your lungs

Each of your lungs is structured like a great tree with many branches ending in tiny twigs. The bronchi, the two main airways branching off the windpipe, divide again and again to form ever smaller passages called bronchioles. The smallest bronchioles are narrower than hairs. They lead to microscopic air sacs called alveoli.

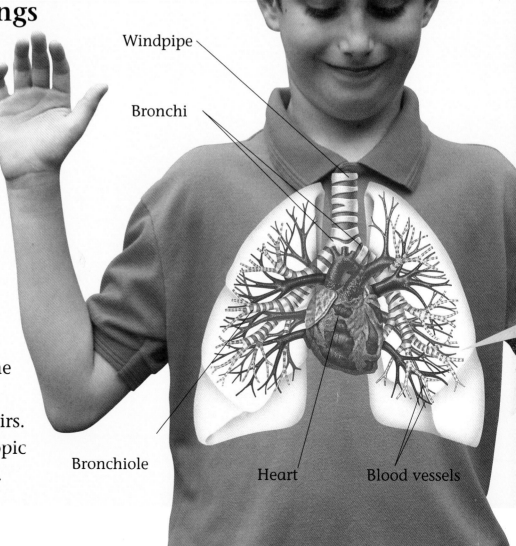

Windpipe

Bronchi

Bronchiole

Heart

Blood vessels

10

Listen to your lungs

If you ask a friend to listen carefully, they may be able to hear the sounds that your lungs are making. If you find it difficult to breathe, it's important that you visit a doctor for advice. Doctors use an instrument called a stethoscope to make it easier to hear the breath sounds.

Air passages

The trachea (windpipe) leading from your throat to the bronchi is supported by a number of C-shaped rings of rubbery cartilage (below). These rings hold your windpipe open and make it tough and flexible. The rings prevent your trachea from being damaged if it gets knocked.

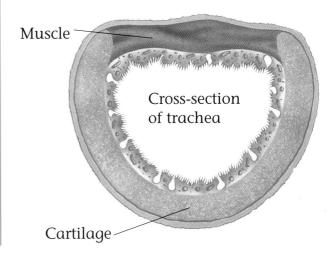

Muscle

Cross-section of trachea

Cartilage

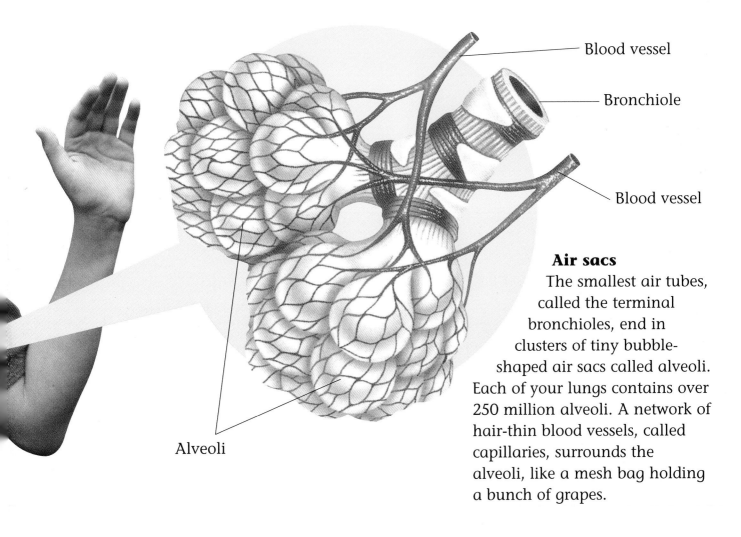

Blood vessel

Bronchiole

Blood vessel

Alveoli

Air sacs

The smallest air tubes, called the terminal bronchioles, end in clusters of tiny bubble-shaped air sacs called alveoli. Each of your lungs contains over 250 million alveoli. A network of hair-thin blood vessels, called capillaries, surrounds the alveoli, like a mesh bag holding a bunch of grapes.

Breathing in and out

The physical process of breathing is powered by two main types of muscles—the intercostal muscles that lie between your ribs, and a flat, curving sheet of muscle attached to the bottom of your rib cage, called the diaphragm. The combined contraction (tightening) and relaxing of these muscles changes the volume of your lungs. Air is sucked in to fill the extra space and forced out again when your lungs return to their original size.

A child's lungs can normally hold about 1.5 quarts/liters of air. If you breathe in very deeply, you can hold about 3 quarts/liters! Adults can hold up to 5 quarts/liters.

Measure your breathing

Ask a friend to measure your chest after you have taken a deep breath to fill your lungs with air. Then measure your chest again after emptying your lungs. The difference between the two measurements represents how much your rib cage expands as you breathe.

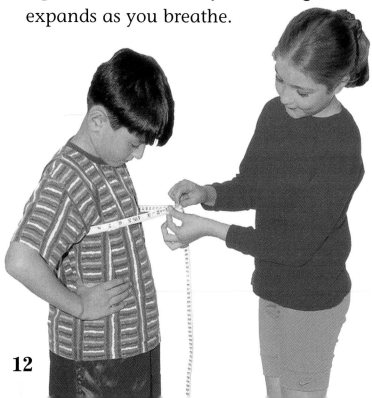

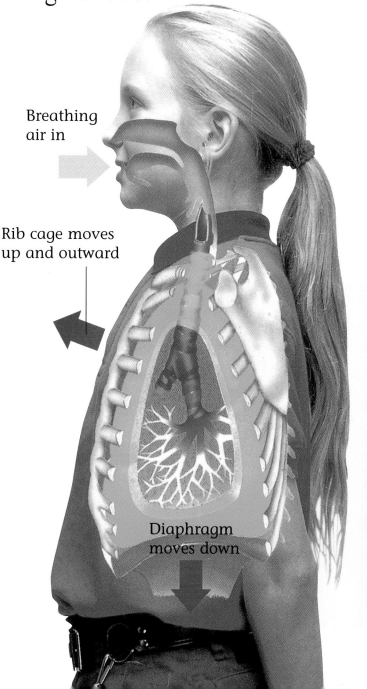

Breathing air in

Rib cage moves up and outward

Diaphragm moves down

Moving cage

The flexible cage of your ribs expands when you suck air into your lungs. When you breathe out, your ribs move downward and inward to make the space inside smaller, forcing air out. You can feel your ribs rising and falling gently as you breathe normally. Now try jogging on the spot for a minute, and feel them again.

Blowing

When you blow up a balloon, you fill it with air from your lungs. Each out-breath makes the balloon a little larger. If you get a bit dizzy when you are blowing up balloons, it is because you are over-breathing—the feeling will soon go away if you stop blowing and rest for a while.

Breathing air out

Breathe easy

If you feel short of breath after exercise, lean forward with your hands on your knees. Muscles in your neck, shoulder, chest, and stomach aid your breathing muscles in this position, to help you "catch your breath."

Rib cage moves down and inward

Breathing muscles

When you breathe in, your intercostal muscles tighten, pulling the ribs outward to stretch your lungs, and your diaphragm contracts, pulling the lungs down. Air is sucked in to fill this extra space in your lungs. When the breathing muscles relax, the lungs shrink back to their former size, forcing the air out again.

Diaphragm moves up

Breathe in

Ribs

Breathe out

What happens when you breathe?

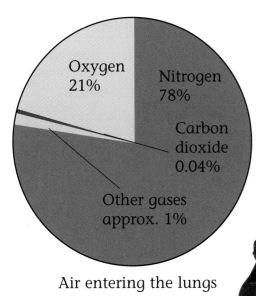

Escape artist Harry Houdini (1874-1926) trained himself to hold his breath so that he could perform daring underwater escapes.

When you breathe, oxygen from the air passes through the lining of the alveoli into your blood. Your cells use this oxygen to break down food molecules and to produce the energy you need to keep going. The waste product of this process, carbon dioxide, seeps into the blood and returns to the lungs where you breathe it out.

Gases in the lungs

When you breathe, the mixture of gases in your lungs changes. Incoming air contains 21 percent oxygen and a tiny amount of carbon dioxide. Outgoing air contains less oxygen and more carbon dioxide. The main gas in air, nitrogen, is not used by your body.

Being knocked out of breath

A blow to the stomach forces air out of your lungs, making you gasp. The diaphragm may also spasm briefly, stopping the lungs from filling with air.

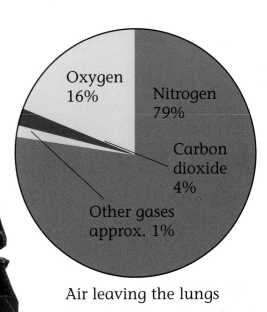

Oxygen 21%
Nitrogen 78%
Carbon dioxide 0.04%
Other gases approx. 1%

Air entering the lungs

Oxygen 16%
Nitrogen 79%
Carbon dioxide 4%
Other gases approx. 1%

Air leaving the lungs

14

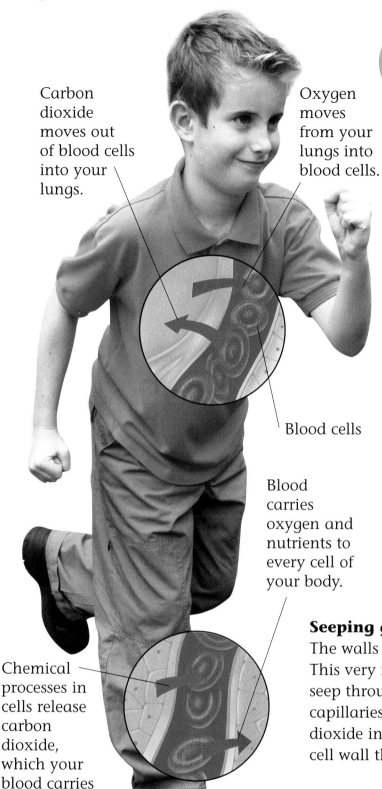

Carbon dioxide moves out of blood cells into your lungs.

Oxygen moves from your lungs into blood cells.

Blood cells

Blood carries oxygen and nutrients to every cell of your body.

Chemical processes in cells release carbon dioxide, which your blood carries back to the lungs.

Mouth to mouth

The air you breathe out still contains quite a lot of oxygen. You can help to get an injured person's lungs working again by giving them oxygen from your breath, using mouth-to-mouth resuscitation (shown below, being practiced on a dummy).

Seeping gases

The walls of the alveoli are only about one cell thick. This very fine barrier allows oxygen in the alveoli to seep through the cell wall and into the blood capillaries, where it is carried around the body. Carbon dioxide in the bloodstream seeps through the alveoli cell wall the other way, so you can breathe it out.

Carbon dioxide in the blood

Carbon dioxide leaving the alveoli

Oxygen entering the alveoli

Oxygen in the blood

Exchange of gases

Your heart pumps oxygen-rich blood around your body. Your cells use this oxygen when they break down your food. The waste product, carbon dioxide, can be harmful if it builds up in your body. Instead, it moves from your blood to your lungs where it is breathed out.

15

Producing sounds

When singing, you reach high and low notes by tightening or loosening the vocal cords in your throat.

As well as taking in vital oxygen, breathing also allows you to talk, so you can communicate with others. You speak using the vocal cords in your throat and also your lips, teeth, and tongue. Your breathing equipment also helps you to produce other sounds—such as singing, shouting, humming, and whistling. You breathe out in different ways to express your emotions, as you laugh, sob, or sigh.

Speech equipment

Your larynx, or voice box, contains the vocal cords which make sounds. Your larynx lies at the top of your windpipe. As you breathe out, air passing up the windpipe vibrates the vocal cords to produce sounds. You shape these sounds into words using your cheeks, lips, teeth, and tongue.

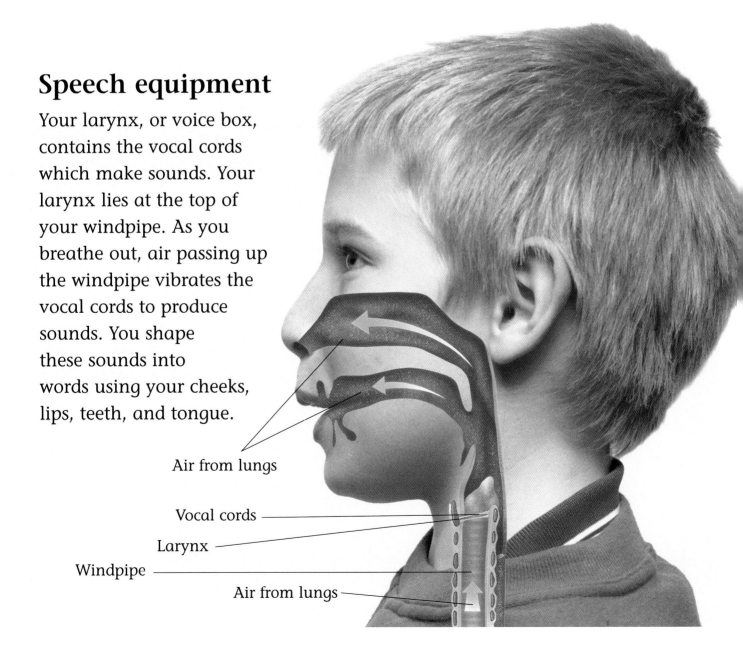

Air from lungs

Vocal cords

Larynx

Windpipe

Air from lungs

Sounding hoarse

If you strain your voice by shouting, your vocal cords become swollen. They can't vibrate properly and air may leak between your vocal cords when they tighten. This makes you sound hoarse. Resting your voice will help to reduce the swelling.

Vocal cords

Your vocal cords are two stretchy flaps or shelves attached to the voice box (larynx) and supported by muscles. Normally, a wide gap between the cords allows air to pass through without making a noise. When you speak or sing, the vocal cords tighten and the gap between them closes. Air passing up the windpipe now vibrates the cords to produce sounds.

Larynx

Windpipe

Vocal cords

Sinuses

The sinuses are a series of small, hollow chambers inside your head, connected to your nasal cavity. They are lined with mucus which helps to moisten the air that you breathe. When you talk, sounds echo in your sinuses. If you have a cold and your sinuses become inflamed or blocked, your voice will sound very different.

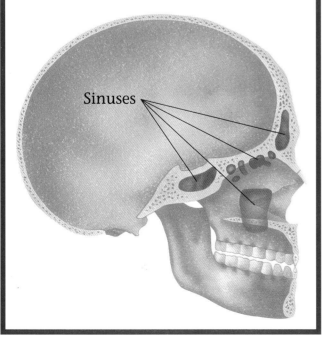

Sinuses

You make your voice louder or softer to shout, scream, or whisper by adjusting the force of the air you breathe out.

Clearing the airways

When you sneeze, air whooshes out of your nostrils at up to 100 mph (160 kph)—as fast as the winds in a hurricane.

The delicate tissue of your lungs is easily damaged by dust, smoke, and pollution. Luckily, your breathing system has several built-in safety features that prevent "foreign bodies" from reaching the lungs. Sticky fluid (mucus) and tiny hairs (cilia) help to trap and collect dirt so that your body can clear them from your breathing passages.

Cilia hairs

Mucus gland

Coughs and sneezes

Coughing and sneezing help to clear dust, dirt, mucus, and germs from your airways. When you cough, air rushes up your windpipe and out of your mouth, rattling your vocal cords on the way. A sneeze clears the upper airways by blasting air from your nose.

Spreading germs
When you sneeze, you send a mist of fine mucus and germs spraying up to ten feet (three meters) away. Always use a handkerchief when you sneeze, and put your hand over your mouth when you cough.

Hairy passages

Your nostrils are lined with hairs that filter dirt and dust to prevent them from entering your body. Your windpipe and nasal cavity are lined with smaller hairs called cilia (above). These move in waves to sweep up dirty mucus, so it can be swallowed, or coughed, or sneezed out.

Snoring

You may snore when you're asleep if the air you breathe in rattles the soft palate in your mouth, or the flap that hangs there (the uvula). Some people snore if they lie on their back or have a blocked nose. Lying on your side and raising your head with pillows can help.

Hiccups

A hiccup is a sudden intake of air that occurs when your diaphragm tightens more strongly than usual. The in-breath snaps the epiglottis in your throat, producing a loud "hic." Hiccups can usually be cured by sipping water slowly or by holding your breath.

Choking

If your food goes down your windpipe and you start to choke, you will usually be able to dislodge the obstruction by coughing. Very rarely a piece of food can completely block the windpipe. If this happens, an adult can help you to breathe by performing the "Heimlich maneuver." This involves clasping under your diaphragm and squeezing suddenly—which forces out a blast of air to free the obstruction.

Germ-eaters

Your body has a certain type of blood cell, called macrophages, that fights germs and infections in the lungs and other parts of the body. These microscopic cells wander around the body in search of germs and then surround and destroy them.

Breathing rates

When you go jogging, your lungs and heart have to work harder to supply your muscles with oxygen than when you are lounging in a comfy chair.

Your body needs less oxygen when you are resting than when you are doing something energetic, such as running or cycling. Your brain automatically adjusts your breathing rate to suit your body's changing needs. At rest, your muscles don't use any oxygen, so your breathing is slow and shallow. When you run or cycle, your muscles need lots of oxygen, so your breathing muscles work hard to pump air into your lungs.

Getting a stitch

A stitch, or cramp in your side, is a mysterious pain that may be linked to your diaphragm. You may get a stitch if you exercise too soon after eating. This may be caused if the diaphragm doesn't get enough oxygen when the stomach is digesting.

Measure your breathing rates

When you rest, you breathe in about 0.5 quarts/liters of air with each breath, and take about 12 breaths a minute. When you run you breathe faster and deeper, breathing in up to 4 quarts/liters of air with each breath, and breathing up to 60 times a minute. This means you take in 40 times as much air! Try counting your breaths as you rest, walk, and run.

Sleeping

Walking

20

Brain power

Your brain works best when it has a ready supply of oxygen—that's why it's difficult to think in a warm, stuffy room! The respiratory center at the base of your brain is also used to gather information about oxygen levels in your blood, to instruct your breathing muscles to work harder if necessary. All this happens automatically, without your having to think about it. Alternatively, you can adjust your breathing yourself, by holding your breath, for example.

Nerve center

Nerves carry messages

Respiratory muscles

Running

Yawning

Yawning is an automatic reflex that is probably caused by shallow breathing. We don't know why people yawn. It seems to happen more when people are tired or have been sleeping. It may just be a way of stretching the rib cage after resting. It's also catching! If you see your friend yawn, you may start yawning yourself!

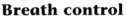

Breath control

When you sing or play a wind instrument, you adjust your breathing to fit the pattern of the music. Blowing harder or softer can increase or decrease the volume of the sound. When you play the flute, you can produce different notes by varying the angle of the breath that you blow into the instrument.

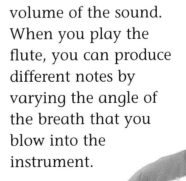

Fresh air, dirty air

In order to survive, everyone needs to breathe clean, fresh air continuously. However, in some parts of the world, such as crowded cities or industrial centers, the air is not very clean. Smoke and fumes given off by factories, power stations, and cars pollute (dirty) the air and can cause breathing problems. Some people also damage their lungs and airways by smoking cigarettes.

Smoking

Smoking is bad for your breathing system and your general health. The smoke from cigarettes irritates the lining of your lungs, which makes extra mucus to try and clear away the smoke particles. Smoking also damages the cilia hairs that clear mucus away from the lungs. Smokers develop a cough because they are unable to clear this extra mucus naturally. Smoking can also damage the structure of the lungs and increase the risk of developing serious illnesses, such as heart disease, lung cancer (right), and emphysema.

Dangerous jobs
Some jobs involve working where the air is dirty. Coal miners and quarry workers regularly breathe in air that is polluted by coal or rock dust. Workers in the food industry can also breathe in fine particles such as flour (above). Nowadays, care is taken to protect workers from the effects of air pollution.

City smog

Some cities are covered in a dirty haze called "smog." City dwellers may develop breathing problems if the polluted air irritates their airways. Mexico City (shown right, on a clear day) is one of the world's most polluted cities. On a smoggy day, visibility is less than half a mile and you can't see the tops of these buildings or the mountains.

Mountain air

Mountain air is generally clean and healthful because mountains are far from cities and factories that create pollution. However, the air at high altitudes contains less oxygen. Mountain climbers sometimes have to breathe oxygen carried in special cylinders.

Car fumes

Cars and trucks give off a mixture of poisonous exhaust gases, including carbon monoxide. This dangerous gas makes the blood less able to carry oxygen, causing breathlessness. Many cyclists in traffic-filled cities wear masks that screen out these fumes.

When breathing is difficult

Asthma and allergies are common conditions affecting the lungs and airways, making it difficult to breathe. If you have asthma, your airways sometimes become inflamed and swollen, causing wheezing and shortness of breath. Asthma and allergies can often be treated with medications, but severe asthma can be a serious condition.

Many people are allergic to animals like cats and dogs. An allergy to animal fur, feathers, or skin can make you sneeze or wheeze.

Asthma

If you have asthma you may wheeze, feel short of breath, or have a tight feeling in your chest. These symptoms arise if the walls of the airways become swollen and the airway muscles tighten, making your airways narrower. Breathing asthma medicine into your lungs (using an inhaler) can help open the airways and also prevent symptoms.

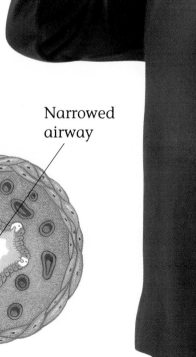

Normal airway

Narrowed airway

Allergies

If you suffer from allergies, you may react to normally harmless substances, like dust, pollen, and fur. Your airways may become irritated and swollen; your eyes, throat, and nasal passages may become sore and itchy; and your nose may run. Nasal sprays and medicines called antihistamines can reduce the inflammation caused by allergies.

Tiny culprits

Even clean, fresh air contains tiny particles of dust, pollen grains, and bits of fur and feathers. These particles can trigger asthma and other allergies. Dust mites, (left, shown magnified) are tiny creatures that live in dust and bedding materials. Their powdery droppings float in the air and can trigger an allergic reaction.

Keep active

Having asthma or allergies need not prevent you from playing sports or doing strenuous exercise. Just be aware of your breathing, and make sure you carry your medicine with you at all times. Before strenuous exercise, warm up slowly and cool down afterward. If you often feel short of breath during exercise, talk to your doctor or nurse about how to keep asthma from spoiling your fun.

Hay fever

Hay fever is an allergy to pollen that is released by grass and other flowering plants during the spring and summer. The tiny pollen grains that fill the air can irritate the nose, eyes, and throat, particularly on dry, breezy days.

Lungs for life

A baby's lungs develop before birth, but it doesn't take its first breath of air until it is born. The moment you are born, your lungs start breathing to supply your body with oxygen. This process continues day in, day out, every minute of your life. As you get older, your lungs grow and change along with the rest of your body.

Exercising regularly helps to strengthen your breathing muscles and keep your lungs in top condition. But know your limits—don't overdo it!

Placenta

Umbilical cord

Developing lungs

Before birth, a developing baby grows in a liquid-filled sac. It gets oxygen and nourishment from its mother, through the placenta and umbilical cord. When it is born, a baby's lungs are miraculously ready to take in air and provide oxygen for the baby.

First breaths

Just after birth, your lungs filled with air for the first time, and oxygen started to reach your blood from the alveoli. Young babies breathe very quickly, taking 40 to 50 breaths per minute. This breathing rate gradually slows down to about 25 breaths per minute by the time you are five years old. Some newborn babies need a ventilator (right) to help them to breathe.

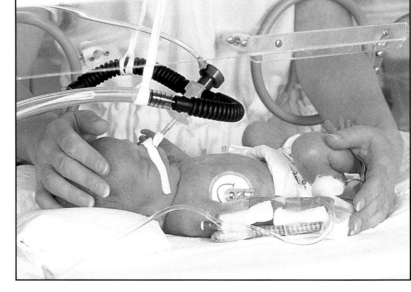

Passive smoking

Even if you don't smoke, your lungs can still be damaged by smoky air if you come into regular contact with other people's cigarette smoke. This is called passive smoking. Encourage friends and family to give up smoking for your sake, as well as their own!

Keep your lungs active

When you exercise, you take more air into your lungs to give your cells the extra oxygen they need. This helps to strengthen your breathing muscles. Walking is one of the easiest exercises to do every day—even as you get older!

Breathing oxygen

The air around you contains about one-fifth oxygen. People who are having difficulty breathing are sometimes given extra oxygen through a tube inserted in their nose, which they breathe along with normal air. In more serious cases a face mask may be used.

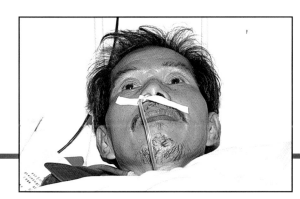

85 Years
50%

65 Years
62%

45 Years
82%

Up to 25 years
Full capacity

Human lung capacity
at different ages

Absorbing oxygen

The lungs of newborn babies are not fully developed. The alveoli continue to develop until you are about eight years old. After the age of 25 years, your lungs gradually become less able to absorb oxygen.

Keeping healthy

During a major outbreak of flu in 1918, some people wore army gas masks to avoid catching the disease.

The pair of lungs you are born with have to last you right through life. It's vital to take as much care of your breathing system as you can. Eating a balanced diet and taking regular exercise will help to keep your lungs and breathing muscles healthy. Protect your lungs from harmful pollution by avoiding cigarette smoke and other fumes.

Fighting infection

Colds and flu are spread by coughs and sneezes. They can sometimes lead to chest infections if they spread to the lungs. Colds and flu can be difficult to avoid, but eating a healthy, balanced diet (with lots of fruit and vegetables) and getting a good night's sleep can help your body to fight off infections.

Stretch and relax

Yoga is a form of exercise that helps you to relax mentally while stretching your joints and muscles. Yoga techniques also involve breath control. For this reason, they are particularly good exercises for anyone with lung and airway problems.

28

Clean air

In built-up areas, car exhaust fumes are a major cause of pollution. Car fumes can irritate the lining of your airways and may cause

breathing problems. Bike riding, walking, or using public transportation, instead of a car, can help reduce traffic congestion and pollution in your area.

Eating for breathing

Doctors now think that a diet rich in fruit and vegetables may help you avoid breathing problems. Researchers have found that foods rich in vitamin C and E can protect against damage to body tissue, such as the lining of the airways.

Get moving!

Regular exercise is good for your heart, your breathing system, and your whole body. You don't have to be keen on sports to take exercise. Walking the dog, dancing, or even walking to school can all count as exercise!

A dangerous habit

Many people start smoking when they are young and wish they had never started when they get older. Don't feel pressured to smoke, even if all your friends light up. As well as being bad for your health, smoking is also very expensive! It's best never to start smoking, but if you do smoke, why not talk to your doctor for help on how to stop.

Breathing check

If you find that you have difficulty with your breathing, talk to an adult about it. A visit to the doctor can easily identify the problem. Your doctor may ask you to blow as hard as you can into a device called a "peak flow meter." This measures how hard you can blow air out of your lungs.

Amazing facts

Most people can only hold their breath for about a minute. Whales and dolphins can hold their breath for much longer.
A diving sperm whale can hold its breath for about two hours!

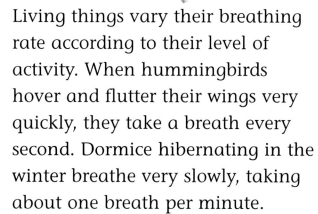

Deep-sea divers breathe a special mixture of gases underwater, including helium, which makes the voice get squeaky. Divers' air tubes are strengthened by tough rings, which work like the rings of rubbery cartilage in your windpipe.

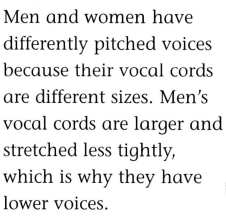

Living things vary their breathing rate according to their level of activity. When hummingbirds hover and flutter their wings very quickly, they take a breath every second. Dormice hibernating in the winter breathe very slowly, taking about one breath per minute.

Men and women have differently pitched voices because their vocal cords are different sizes. Men's vocal cords are larger and stretched less tightly, which is why they have lower voices.

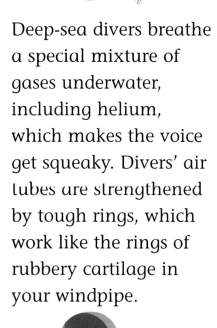

Air rushes out of your lungs at more than 62 mph (100 kph) when you cough—as fast as highway traffic!

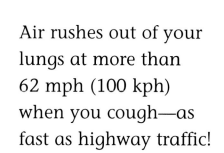

Glossary

alveoli [sing. alveolus] The microscopic air sacs in the lungs through which oxygen passes into the bloodstream, and carbon dioxide in the blood passes into the lungs.

bronchi [sing. bronchus] The main airways that branch off from the windpipe and lead to the lungs.

bronchioles The smaller air tubes that branch off from the bronchi and narrow down to end in tiny air sacs in the lungs.

cilia The tiny hairs in the airways that sweep dirt and mucus upward to keep the lungs clean.

diaphragm The large, flat muscle attached to the bottom of your rib cage, that is used in breathing.

intercostal muscles The muscles, lying between the ribs, that expand and shrink the rib cage to draw air in and out of the lungs.

larynx The voice box in the throat, containing the vocal cords that produce speech and other sounds.

mucus A sticky fluid, made by the lining of the airways, that traps dust and dirt to keep the lungs clean.

nasal cavity A hollow chamber inside the head leading from the nostrils to the throat.

oxygen An invisible gas found in the air that almost all animals need to survive.

respiration The exchange of oxygen and carbon dioxide between the air and the lungs, blood, and body cells.

respiratory system All the body parts involved in breathing, including the nose, mouth, windpipe, and lungs.

trachea The windpipe, which links the throat with the bronchi and lungs.

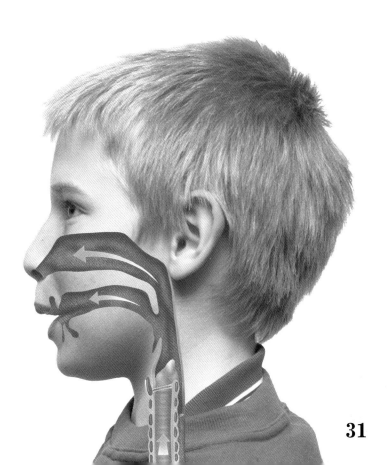

Index

Photo credits

Abbreviations: l-left, r-right, b-bottom, t-top, c-center, m-middle

All photos supplied by Select Pictures except for: 4tr—Corel. 7bl—Karl Weatherly / CORBIS. 15mr—Blarie Seitz / Science Photo Library. 22mr, 25mr—Corbis. 22bm—Department of Clinical Radiology, Salisbury District Hospital / Science Photo Library. 23tr—Photodisc. 26bm—Publiphoto Diffusion / Science Photo Library. 27ml—A. Crump, TDR, WHO / Science Photo Library. 27tr—Hughes Martin / CORBIS. 29tm—Mark Clarke/Science Photo Library. 29mr—National Asthma Campaign.